CW01095757

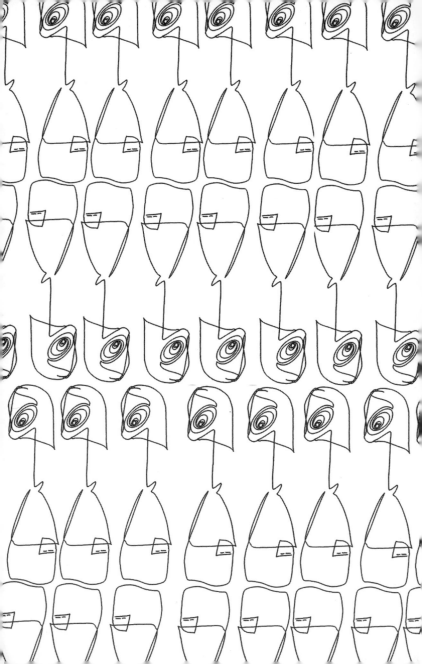

Rain Dancers in the Data Cloud

William Stephenson

Templar Poetry

First Published 2012 by Templar Poetry

Fenelon House
Kingsbridge Terrace
58 Dale Road, Matlock, Derbyshire
DE4 3NB
www.templarpoetry.co.uk

ISBN 9781906285920

Copyright © William Stephenson 2012

Typeset by Pliny
Cover Design Artwork by Jane Weir
Printed and bound in India

To June, Bob and Jim

Acknowledgements

Some of these poems, or earlier versions of them, have already appeared in the following magazines: *Anon, Envoi, The North, Obsessed with Pipework, Pennine Platform* and *Sentinel Literary Quarterly*.

Contents

Building the New School

They believe in girders and breeze-blocks:
in netting awaiting camouflage,
in scaffolding lit up
like the gantry at Cape Canaveral.
They trust in the ululating summons
of a tungsten twist-bit grinding steel:
in swarf smouldering in helical curls
as the filings blaze a comet-trail.

They swear by posters in Urdu and English:
Lend Lease. Improving the Image of Construction.
These signs puzzle the watchman from Poznan
who slides his tongue round each awkward syllable
in *Hard Hat Area* and *Report to Security*
as he fingers a pound coin
till the milled edge darkens with his dead skin
and the Queen grows slick with sweat and nicotine.

Meanwhile, hammers beat time into the night.
Floodlights bolted to the perimeter fence
turn the watchman's cigarette fumes white
as he stamps his feet, spits phlegm
and rubs his change, counting imaginary dollars,
rehearsing such English as the school supplies:
Releasing Potential, Achieving Excellence.
Patrolled By Dogs. Strictly No Admittance.

The Future of Personal Computing

The pentahydrate sits in fifty-kilo burlap sacks
stacked like bombs awaiting a bay. We sweated
all yesterday, humping the last batch to a hole
twenty metres from a village well.
The fibres peel our skin, but it pays.
The stencilling says *Use no hooks*. Of course
I read that myself. I can speak bloody English:
I'm the boss's number two. I'm saving for college.

In Impact forty-eight point, our website shrieks
We lock, we track, we bag every single part.
The boss pasted it from a commercial for motorbikes.
I funnel memory chips into polythene bags
like evidence on *CSI: Miami* (yes, we have
Sky here), stuff ruined towers into bin liners
then hurl the lot into the crusher. I'm learning
my symbols. Silicon, mercury, lead: Si, Hg, Pb.

See all these plastic lattices? The skeletons
of hard-working keyboards. RIP. Emails,
reports, letters, diaries and novels broke them,
hammered out by fingers tapping spastically
like a Taser hit that lasts hours. Got the camera?
I'll hold one up. *Pause, Break, Home, End,*
Control, Shift, Caps Lock, Tab. The sun
shines right through the holes. *Escape.*

Angels in the Architraves

Gaudí's holy theme-park; the roof-terrace
at La Pedrera. *The pinnacle of Catalan architecture,*
fanfares your brochure: *the pride of Barcelona.*
But to you, it's Hammer Horror: air-vents
twisty as vipers; the parapet's switchback dip;
chimney-cowls sculpted into masks that glower
at the tourists who clamber with the chutzpah of lemurs.

The audacious architect argued with the budget-holders;
few understood how krakens, horns and devil-masks
could embellish an up-market apartment block. Seeking
salvation in hydraulics, he ripped out the staircase,
installed elevators; had *Ave Maria Gratia Plena*
cemented onto the façade. But to admire his prayer
you must teeter six storeys above the boulevard . . .

No. One glance twists your inner garrotte.
So, faithless empiricist, you focus on the proximate:
your trainers, still soggy with the morning's rain;
the ground-down butt of a Gitane; an effete silhouette
that's either your shadow or Gaudí's spirit
watching us unbelievers scuttle across his vision
like a migrant termite hive, anoraks heavy as chitin.

At the Cathedral Bell-Tower, Florence

No Entry to Persons with Conditions of the Heart!
Jesus, they mean it – yours kicks like a foetus
as you labour up the staircase,
a dark helix quarried into the granite.
Tunnels narrow to capillaries – daylight's so distant
it must be fiction. *Scusi! Pardon.* A school party
shuffles down; Reeboks rasp on stone.

Then a ghost, shawled in hessian, ices your shoulder;
George Eliot, last seen here 1861; still on her leisurely
Grand Tour, busy plotting *Romola*, she glides
through our backpacks, cameras, *I Heart Italy* hats.
She fills the tunnel, her crinoline brushing both walls
as she scans each sandal-worn flight like a sentence,
ascending turn by turn into the Renaissance.

You reach the roof together. To you, everyday anarchy
unspools below: tourists whirl in the piazza's bonfire;
phone-wires thrum as the wind warbles off-key;
whereas Eliot, abstracted,
gazes into a grid as old as print, binds a city-state
between the covers of her memory – a mind-set republic
that scorched heretics but bankrolled the painters of angels.

Hard Times and Hard Travellin'

(Will Kaufman sings Woody Guthrie)

A pick the colour of dry blood circles your thumb
like an ageing plaster peeling from a wound.
As you sing, the cyclones of the dustbowl whirl
while the slide shimmers up and down your fretboard –
a bottle on a stream, heady with the fumes
of moonshine, tossed out of a rattling jalopy
by some hicks, prairie dirt leaking from their ears,
seeking cool rivers of silver dollars in California.

The last chord dies and we applaud;
you unclip the capo and the strings relax.
You stick a sign to the sound-board: This Machine
Kills Fascists. Woody, smiling grainily
in digitally-enhanced sepia, stares down
from PowerPoint heaven, fingers spread over his guitar;
a saint waving a benediction, or the president
of an invisible republic whose decrees are ballads in D.

With every hammer-on and strum, your strings shudder
like the tickertape machines that ruined Hoover,
bringing news of a suicidal run on shares –
because like us, Woody lived among crashes, fire,
brokers jumping from high windows. As he hoboed
from state to state, he passed old men chewing tobacco,
watching the ashes of America blow over: There goes
Kansas. Yep. That there cloud was Oklahoma.

The Shape-Changer

for Robert Owens Greygrass

In Lakota, his name crackles like a fire –
but in English, it's soft and bitter as ash.
He says his stories, too, must wither in translation,
like game dried for winter. Then, Protean,
he talks his way into feathers, skins, fur.

Fingers forked like a tongue, he's a boy
who wriggles away hissing when his mother speaks –
so the medicine-man hacks off his limbs,
drags him to a brake thick with fallen leaves
and binds his new scales tight over his skin.

Eyes peeping over his forearm, he's a wolf
behind a log, deep in snow, watching a hunter
gut a hare. He crawls under the gun,
but the hunter grins, throws him a strip.
So in return, he whispers see-by-night medicine.

The final skin he enters is his own. At a Sun Dance,
his duty was to feed the fire nine whole days.
The flames drew forms – birds, mountains, trees –
then a young girl who wore his wife's eyes.
They named the baby Stands in a Fire Woman.

She's twenty-one now, at college. I was a junky
till she came. She could have been born anywhere
but a hundred lucky chances brought her to me
just like they brought you here. So listen, share.
Wear your skin well. Keep watching the fire.

Half a Million Single Women Live in Beijing

his in-flight magazine had whispered:
and as their taxi scurried past an auto-rickshaw,
Yanmei brushed a star from her midnight hair.
He clung to his laptop and mind-Googled
business + trip + affair. Around them surged
the rush-hour's human ocean; bicycle-shoals;
lorry-whales; posters in Mandarin wide as sails.

They swapped gifts: the signed shirt he'd blagged
at Wembley (he'd thought Yanmei a guy's name);
a man-boobed soapstone Buddha. Laughter,
room-service Bollinger: the contract materialized,
he pledged his investment in a blur; then dreamt
a cruise up her Pearl River, while *Flowers of Asia IV*;
Hot Kung Fu Babes streamed across his monitor.

He awoke in his office, eight time-zones away,
picking rice-husks from a pork sweet-and-sour
while the Buddha signed A-OK
with thumb and finger, under a London sky
the no-iron white of the England top he'd given her.
The inbox in his head pinged: *Come back honey.*
China warm business exc. Friends call me Rooney.

In the Wilderlands of Sword and Sorcery

A week into our quest, I was pimping my avatar —
mouse-clicking nicks into my broadsword,
tattooing virtual runes across my thews —
when Sonja the Warrioress, sworn blood-sister, lover,

direct-messaged: *Pls hear: am Chao Li, math professor.*
Prisoner @ China camp. Cd die 4 msgng u. We play
12 hrs str8, guards farm avatars, sell health, game-gold
4 $$$ 2 Euro, US, SEAsia players. Pls post 2 blog.

No way. I'd watched her split orcs with a scimitar,
the graphics-engine churning fractals into her hair;
then we'd lain by the campfire, battle-sweat on skin.
I exit. Wait a game-day. Log in, third-person screen.

No Sonja. *She disappeared @ dawn,* types an archer:
No msg. Whole mission fkd now imho. Sad emoticon.
Enough. I pour a libation, hone my blade on a stone.
Tonight I'll drag the cursor across my scars.

Yoda

So fame finally comes. Body-double in motion
capture suit me plays. In white room he dances;
digi-cam into data him turns. A star
born is! Meanwhile, I my lightsaber swish
in swamps of Dagobah, training Skywalker
who defeat Vader will, yes. Foreseen it I have.

But when Skywalker departed has
I sense Double lonely is. *The check
will reach your agent by Friday, now don't come back*,
they say. Double inside weeps. Feeling
soul's agony, I across time and galaxies leap
to beside him through Wal-Mart system walk.

Sanguinello, Ruby Breakfast, Original Without
Bits: shelved juices mystic names display.
Double up nose white powder snorts;
into mobile at Woman shouts.
Trust me, I whisper. He screams, *Jesus!
Who are...? Please, I'll drop the coke, I swear.*

No, I him assure, *a coal-carrier you are not
but you a heavy burden bear. We Jedi alone
can Terra from clutches of the Dark deliver.*
So I make him flowers buy; give him sweet words
to Woman to speak; push him work to seek.
For prevail we will. The Force strong within us is.

Dreaming in English

Term-time, I study Geology. In summer, Tourism.
Hi, I'm Marco. How can I help? Hi, I'm Marco ...
After nine hours on Reception I watch the evening
seep into the route-map tacked to the lobby wall
and I feel English inundate my mind: an ancient river
depositing its opaque sediment of inflection,
rules untrammelled by logic, random grammar:

I sleeped and dreamed of sheeps ... Actually,
when I dream, I tongue that sucked-lemon 'i'
the Brits form effortlessly and the Yanks
warp into their own gum-chew:
fit, hit, wit. But awake, I stumble into
feet, heat, wheat. My Latin vowels squeak:
a jammed turnstile, shutting me out of the game.

English is essential for an academic career,
my thesis instructor declared (in Italian)
while skimming an illustrated article
about the mesas of Arizona: *Like colossal
pyramid temples*, burbled the author –
but I saw only the phonemes of an imperial
idiom, dust in eddies whirling between.

Corporate Hospitality

The wallpaper's brilliant – surplus bumper stickers
from the A1 Print Emporium. Coca-Cola Classic,
a font like waves. Dunlop, black on yellow,
bold italics straining against the hand-brake.
Tea? Mind your head – the ceiling's concrete.
The underbelly of Independence Bridge. Touch it –
that's the rush-hour traffic shaking your hand.
The floor's tarpaulin, fixed with bent skewers
Dad fished from a skip behind the Bosporus Kebab House.

Sometimes a container truck from the docks
thunders over and blasts us all awake.
Anandamayi bitches and swears till Mum says
Shh, your father has work. Look, I can spell *Nike,
Ninja, Nintendo.* Nike is the Goddess of Victory.
Mr Chao lets me surf Wiki in afternoon recess –
he says I'm so smart I can winkle myself out
from under this bridge, find a sponsor downtown.
Then Delhi, Singapore, Harvard, who knows?

Like my calendar? The man in the space suit
is Buzz Aldrin. Suspended in the vacuum
above Buzz's Lunar Buggy are five tyres
ranked by size, from moped-grade up to the best,
the Eagle F1. This morning, I crossed off yesterday

on Buzz's helmet then ran my index finger
over the blue curve of the earth, a light-second away,
where inscribed across the ocean, from here to Zanzibar,
is Good Year. Dad says he likes that. It's been one so far.

The Man Who Became A Syndicated Strip

It's funny. The day I went national,
my skin shrivelled into newspaper;
I felt an outline, where body met air, sharpen
by the hour. Now, I can no longer walk or run:
one frame, I'm in the corridor; the next,

talking to you here, my every syllable stuffed
into an inflated comma that floats over my head,
its tail pointing to my lips. The second I speak,
I white out a circle of wall or door; think,
and smoke-signals puff from my hair;

asterisks, exclamation-marks and ampersats
jostle when I swear. But the real nightmare
is inspiration. A hundred-watt bulb flares
above my bald patch, yellowing the air;
in case you miss it, the letters scream *IDEA!*

So what's this interview for? Yes, I'm here;
but should I talk to you or ink the bubbles in?
Are you scratching my errors with a rubber?
Will the colourist blot my cheeks crimson?
If I punch you, will *POW!* shoot from a star?

Airbus and Goose

My job ends in February. Anne-Marie won't even
blow me. Jeremy thumbs X-Box, smokes skunk all day.
Our tenth session. Already. Your problems extend
pseudopodia, multiply asexually; petri-dish bacilli.

If I don't listen, they can't infect me. So I prescribe
arbitrary palliatives – jogging, cognitive-behavioural
bubble-wrap – stare through my surgery window
past some avian graffitist's spray-gun logo

and sink into the view: retail park, airport, estuary.
An Airbus rears above the runway, a fat silver dildo.
A goose flaps at the tip of a migrating arrow.
Am I the dildo or the bird, I wonder, almost

audibly, before damming that dark tributary
to gaze instead at the tin roofs of PC World
and ASDA, that after the latest shower
an acid sun is electroplating silver.

Glioblastoma Multiforme

A month after sixty-two, your thoughts refused to.
Your every sentence hung on a subordinate clause;
Thelma and Louise at the cliff, a DVD on pause.

At your case-conference the oncologist
kick-started your stalled inquiry: *years or*
months, with surgery.   It's hard to say.   But don't

drive, anyway.   So you thought, *Stuff the . . .* whatever,
tore up the motorway, litter in the slipstream,
stopped at random, didn't flick your hazards on,

popped your door and waded off the hard shoulder
into a flooded field pearly with a petrol film.
Ripples: a lithium sun. That was when your.

Deadheading for Beginners

His pliers snip the rosebud off another
Swan Vesta. He anoints it with Superglue
then dabs it onto a hundred-watt bulb

already darkened by dozens of match-heads
clustered neat as seeds in a sunflower.
He's connected the bulb to an old Motorola:

crocodile-clips, wire dreadlocks, pearls of solder.
The detonator nests between the sacks,
he says. *Not tight; combustion needs oxygen.*

My shed's sandbagged with fertilizer.
I tease out a match, reach for my Bensons:
he shakes his head. Wisdom. He subscribes

to *Scientific American*. Me, I trim hedges.
But tomorrow, I'll transmit the text
that transmutes the City into a rose-bed

and propels the Index into tailspin.
Scraps of suit will drift like dandelion
parachutes; we'll turn manure into a garden.

Lapidary

The mason's chisel cuts an X;
your window smashed on *Kristallnacht*.
Now an H; transit-camp wire taut
between poles. A circumflex;

the rat-ridden barn-annexe
where you shivered under straw
till the *Hauptmann* shot an umlaut
into the backs of your parents' necks.

Einsatzgruppe. Now the scrollwork
traces barbed loops on the border;
an S shapes the meat-hook
that held the rope that choked

your marriage suddenly; an O
the gaping left in you by Sadat's
bullet in '73 (your Kibbutz ambushed
on Yom Kippur: a reluctant Israeli).

Now the mason blows the grit
off your name's final character:
I reach inside your pocket-book to
pay him, as if that closes the matter.

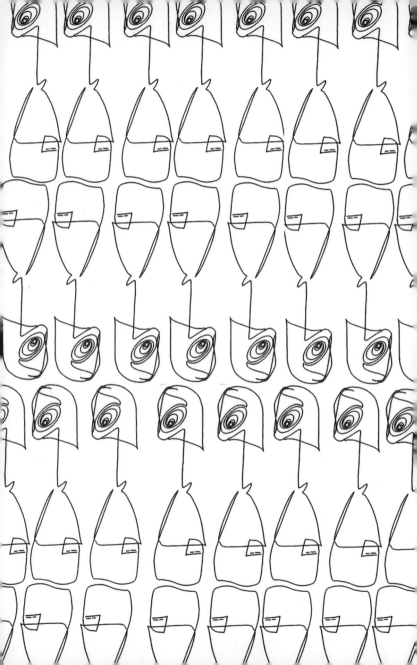

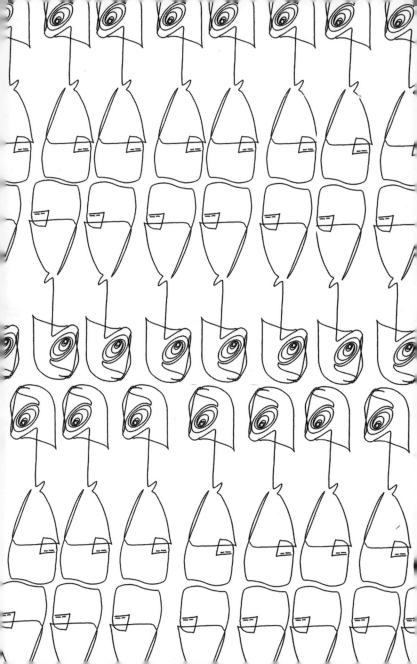